Chapter 1

As he looked up through the clouds, Hugo, The Protector, thought to himself.

The Protector… How long has it been since the king gave me that title? 900? 1000 years?

It had been so long he could hardly remember. There were very few of his kind remaining, who had survived long enough to remember the day his title was bestowed on him. The Elven King, who did not grant titles without sufficient merit, gave it to him on the day they left their home planet of Gavalonia.

Leaving their home was not a choice made in haste. But the Kingdom of Light had been under attack from the evil that lurked on the dark side of the planet. The Darklings had forced them out with relentless, almost non-stop attacks.

The touch on his shoulder brought him out of his thoughts of the past and back to Earth. Where they had since made their home. Standing next to him was his wife, Merrita. She had been his companion since the days of the old planet. In that time, she had been a fierce warrior. Second to one. Hugo. Whom she would fall for, while they built their new home.

Hugo's attention had been brought back to the matter at hand. Before he could say anything to his wife, the front door opened. With an arm full of wood and a gentle smile, Yanella, their daughter came walking through. "Come Yanella. Sit down, we have something that we must tell you." said Merrita.

"What is it Mother?" Yanella asked. Noticing the polished looking, leather case that was sitting on the table. She knew she had never seen it before but something about it was familiar. "What is that?" She asked.

"This?" Hugo said pointing at the case. "This is for you. Actually, you are the only one who can open it. The amulet you wear around your neck, it is the only key ever made. Place it here." He motioned for her to place it near the center. Where there was a faded indentation. She removed the amulet, which had always had a faint green glow. Like that of an emerald. As she came closer to the case, the necklace began getting brighter. By the time she placed it into the indent, the green glow became so bright that all three of them had to look away. After a moment the amulet went dark.

The case, that had not been opened for centuries, made a cracking sound. Then it opened. As if by magic, the lid pulled all the way back to reveal something Yanella had only heard about in the legends and stories. Teokim blades. Blades, she was told, were so rare that she assumed they were a myth. Nothing to put any real stock into. While she looked at them, she noticed something that she did not expect.

As if she knew what to expect.

The blades seemed to be glowing. Although ever so slightly, the sword had a green hue. Similar to that of the amulet. The dagger, however, looked blue, like the ocean under a mid-day sun.

Nobody said anything about glowing blades before. Yanella thought. Just below the swords was a long bow. She recognized the wood right away. Although it was almost as rare as the blades, she had seen it once before. It had been so long she'd almost forgot that it existed. Though, she had never known it to be crafted into a weapon like this. The wood came from Gavalonia, from the heart of the Mezita tree. The strongest wood their people had ever known and stronger than any wood found on Earth. Her first thought was how these weapons would bring in a great price at market. Her second thought was that these weapons needed a skilled warrior to wield them, or the cost would end up being their life.

"OH FATHER!" Yanella exclaimed. "Where did you get these?"

"I would like you to meet Fibmara and Armigen. Forged by trolls of Inner-Earth. Their forge is the only one capable of the heat required to work the metal ore from the meteor. When the meteor crashed on Earth 1000 years ago, it was the first and last time we found the type of metal it produced. You see that jewel in the hilt of Fibmara? Inside that jewel is a single drop of your blood. The Warlock, Myrith, placed a spell on the sword. As for the dagger, Armigen. Myrith took this to the mer-king Triton. His blue blood, said to hold enormous power, was placed in the stones along with another spell. When Myrith returned the blades to me he said that, because of his spells, you were the only one to touch them. They have stayed in this case ever since."

"Now, there is something else you should know…" Hugo paused, knowing what he was about to say would change their lives forever. "Please let me say something without interruption."

A look of concern was growing on Yanellas face. "Okay father, what is it?"

Hugo took a deep breath and braced himself. "What you do know is that we are originally from the planet Gavalonia. What you do not know is that your real Father is the Elven King of that planet, which is in orbit behind the planet the humans call Jupiter."

"WHAT!? What are you talking about? YOU are my father and YOU are my mother!" she screamed as she moved her focus to Merrita. But Merrita was already walking away. She walked over to a bookshelf and picked up a wooden box. Returning to the stunned teenager she places the box in front of Yanella.

"Go ahead, open it." Merritt said. "Inside you will find what is called a Memory Orb. It was used by our ancestors as a way to teach the young, wood elves our history."

Yanella stared at the orb. She noticed that similar to the blades she had just been given, the orb glowed. But this time it was red. She thought to herself.

Did everything from the old world glow?

She reached for the orb. "How does this thing wor--"

As she was about to touch the orb, her new sword and dagger leapt from their scabbards and straight into Yanellas hands. Stunned, the trio stared at each other. Then they finally heard what the blades must've sensed. The throaty guttural roar.

"It's the Darklings!" Yelled Merrita. Grabbing her own sword. Which could've been described as glowing black. Although, it seemed more like it just absorbed all the light around it giving off no reflections at all.

"Damned vampire riders." Muttered Hugo as he picked up his sword and battle axe.

Yanella took a final glance at the orb and decided to put it in the leather pouch on her hip, before they ran outside to face what was coming.

Chapter 2

Kaleev leaned against the tall oak tree. It was late. The sun had set a few hours before. He enjoyed looking down at the village and imagining what was happening in the light he could see through the windows. He thought to himself.

I wonder. How old is she? I'm only 18 Earth summers. She couldn't be older than that, could she? Not at all.

Just as he was turning to leave, a flash of motion, on the left side of the village, caught the corner of his fiery green eyes. With just the slightest squint he immediately recognized the sight of a vampire dragon rider. He became instantly enraged. Before he had another thought, he was already standing at the spot where the vamp had entered the village.

In his current state his vision would become blue and reveal to him any changes in the temperature of his surroundings. With this skill he could track just about anything. Good for him but bad for the vampire, who's feet left almost black footprints anywhere he stepped. Slowly and silently, Kaleev followed the tracks. As he came around the corner of the next hut the footprints just vanished.

Kaleev crouched low and scanned his surroundings, careful to take note of anything out of place. Just then the vampire dropped from the roof aiming straight down to land top of Kaleev. He saw him just in time to roll to his right. As he came back up to his feet his sword and dagger already drawn. Both blades glowing a brilliant emerald green.

The rider slowly drew his similar pair of blades, as if he was savoring the moment before the kill. Once his blades were free of their scabbards, and without any other indication, he charged. Kaleēv lunged to his left, catching the steel of the riders blade with his own. Making a distinct clanging sound that anyone in the village would recognize. Still in the same motion, while pushing the riders blade aside, he was slashing his sword down on the rider. The rider parried, but the momentum carried Kaleēv to his left. The rider slashed out with his dagger faster than Kaleēv expected and cutting into his upper shoulder and ripping his tunic. Kaleēv dropped to a knee and swung his sword at the knees of his assailant. The rider fell to his back and Kaleēv was on him in an instant, driving his glowing green dagger straight into his chest.

With nothing more than a grunt, the rider stared into Kaleēvs eyes with a look that didn't indicate fear, but more of a knowing of what was coming. With a flick of his wrist, Kaleēvs sword pivoted up and came down. Separating the riders head from his shoulders. The only way to truly kill a vampire.

Kaleev heard a footstep behind him followed by a gasp. He whirled around with his sword at the ready. But to his surprise, what he found staring back at him were the most the most beautiful eyes of a deep cobalt blue. He had only seen her from the cover of brush in the forest. He would watch as she went to and from the stream, where the village gets its water and washes their clothes. He noticed she wasn't staring at him, since he was still concealed in the shadow of the hut, but past him at the lifeless body of the now dead vampire. There was a sudden flash behind Kaleev. He didn't react to the flash because that was typical when a vampire's body turned to ash.

When she finally took her eyes of the ground, where the body had just been, she looked at Kaleev and asked. "Are you going to use those," motioning to the sword and dagger still glowing in his hands, "on me now?"

"Oh! No, no, no." He said. Sheathing both weapons as quickly as he could without cutting himself. He hesitated a moment before stepping out into the moonlight.

She gasped again. She had never seen an Elven warrior before. She had only heard the stories her grandfather would tell her, since he was the village mage. She took in Kaleev. His hair, although should have been black as night, was white as snow and hung down to his shoulders. The pupils of his eyes were like that of a cat, other than his ran left to right as opposed to up and down. He wore two earings in each of his pointed ears. He had no nose. Just a slight ridge with two holes underneath, just above his mouth. He was dressed head to toe in deer skin garments. His pants, tunic, and even his soft soled boots. At his waist was a leather belt, which in addition to his weapons, had a leather pouch attached. The tunic was tucked into his pants and the two sides were laced together up the middle. They were loose enough near the top to leave most of his muscled chest bare. She thought about how neat and orderly his outward appearance seemed to be and yet she had just seen him kill a vampire.

He took another step and froze. Then he said, more to himself than to her "I must find his dragon."

"Are you not going to introduce yourself?" She asked.

"Yes, of course. My apologies." He said. "I am Kaleev, son of Hugo The Protector. My family and I live in the forest, to the south." He pointed his hand towards the south. "I would ask your name as well."

"I am Aireonna. Daughter of the late King Yomee and granddaughter of the Green Mage, Sylumm. Welcome to our village."

"Thank you, ma'lady, but if you would excuse me, I must go. I have a dragon to catch!"

Then, without waiting for a response, he vanished. Back into the shadows.

Chapter 3

Hugo reached the door first and put his ear to it. He could hear one of the dragons drawing in a breath. "FIRE!" He shouted, just as Merrita yanked open the trap door in the floor boards. Yanella dropped through first, then Merrita. Hugo, with his shield on his back, came down last.

"Hurry," Merrita whispered. "this way." Elves had very good vision in the dark.

The small tunnel ended about fifty feet behind the rear of the house. Merrita pushed the sticks, moss and dirt out of the way. The tunnel opened behind a small ridge. The family was armed and ready for a battle. They peered over the edge of the ridge.

The roof of the house was on fire. There were six vampires sitting atop six dragons. Hugo was surprised to see eight additional warriors on foot. He had never seen anything like them. Not one part of the black armor was distinguishable against another. Which made the piece covering their heads appear to be one solid piece, with the only holes being for the eyes.

Hugo crept over the ridge and up behind one of the soldiers that was behind the house. With one swing from his battle axe, he crushed his opponents head. Dropping him to the ground… Dead.

Merrita, upon reaching the top of the ridge, jumped high up into the nearest tree. Grabbing a limb and swinging around the trunk. She let go, throwing herself at the nearest dragon, and pulling out her sword. The rider sensed her presence and looked up. He brought his blade up just in time to keep her black blade from cutting his head off.

Yanella had had enough of watching her house burn. As she walked straight down the ridge, toward the nearest vampire, she drew her new sword and dagger. One of the strange foot soldiers took noticed and headed to cut her off. As soon as he was close enough, he lunged at her with his pike. She caught his pike while spinning to the right. She used the momentum to pull the soldier to her while she brought her sword down from a high arc. Her sword barely seemed to notice the body it was slicing through as it traveled from his left shoulder and out his right hip. His two halves did not fall in the same direction.

Moving to his right, around the corner of what was left of their home, Hugo came face to face with three more pike wielding, strange looking soldiers. He had slung his axe across his back and held his dragon scale shield with his left arm. He unsheathed his own glowing green sword with his right hand. The solders immediately noticed him and took their offensive stance. Hugo took a few steps, side to side, trying to gauge their training. They lowered their pikes, looking like they were about to strike.

Behind the soldiers, a large shadow came lurking through the smoke. The head of the dragon broke through the smoke first. Followed by the rider. Hugo thought that he must be the leader of these dragon riders. The dragon began drawing in a large breath, which only meant one outcome.

OH, CRAP! Hugo thought. He dropped down to his knee and held his shield in front of him. Trying to get as much of himself behind the shield as possible. Just as the dragon let loose a blast of sulfur laden fire. Engulfing the entire area, including the foot soldiers, in the blast.

Chapter 4

Merrita rolled away from the dragon to avoid being close enough for it to use its heavy tail on her. All the while keeping both eyes on the dragons' rider. The vampire had confidence against the female elf, especially while on top of his dragon. But he wasn't so sure about the blade she was wielding so deftly. Unknown to Merrita, the sword the vampire was using was coated with a particular poison. A poison so powerful that it would kill a human on contact. If an elf came in contact it would take 3 days to be fatal, due to the elves natural ability to defend against all foreign toxins.

Merrita summersaulted into the air as the rider slid down his dragons' tail. Their swords clashed the moment his feet touched the ground. The vampire swung his sword at her. She dodged to her left causing the vampire to miss his intended target. Merrita took a few steps back trying to find an opening in the vampires' defense.

The snap of a twig, just as an arrow flew by her head, made her jerk around expecting another attack coming from behind her. The fletchings, she noticed, were from Yanellas arrow. That was all the opportunity the vampirewas looking for. He lunged at her with his sword out, catching her in her left side. The sword sliced through her tunic only barley catching her skin.

Wincing in pain Merrita parried, fending off his next attack. The vampire looked as if he was about to go in for the kill when there were two long horn blasts. The sound was unmistakable as a Fennarious Tooth Horn. It came from a great cat-like creature from their home planet Gavalonia. The creature had been extinct for 500 years.

Merrita, looking a little pale, risked a glance behind her, again. The shaft of an arrow protruded from another vampires' head. With the sweep of her hand, Yanella removed the vampires' head from his torso. In a flash of bright white, his body turned to ash. All that remained was his sword and her arrow, where the head should have been. Hearing the horn, the vampires, their dragons and what remained of the foot soldiers, were gone in an instant.

Hugo peaked out from behind his shield to see what remained of the soldiers turned to ash. He looked up and saw Merrita with a faint smile on her face. "Well, that was interesting." He said. Her smile faltered, replaced with pain, and she collapsed to her knees. He leapt and was at her side in an instant. He caught her before she made it all the way to the ground. "Merrita?" He said, picking her up. He noticed the cut in her tunic and quickly carried her to the small stream nearby. He rinsed out her wound but it didn't look very deep.

Yanella walked over to where the vampire had turned to ash and picked up his sword. "Careful with that!" He barked. "I've seen this type of wound before. She's been poisoned by whatever is coating the blade of that sword." Letting a little frustration seep into his words he said "What in the world is keeping Kaleev?"

Chapter 5

Kaleev crept up to the forests edge. He felt the unusual sensation that he was being watched. That's when a female voice spoke. Only, it was inside his head.

"Elf. For a race that is supposed to be almost silent, you are very noisy."

I gotta be hearing things. He thought.

"NO ELF!" she said. "You are not hearing things."

"Then who are you?"

"My name is Patearum, I am the dragon that you are searching for."

"I am not looking for a dragon." Kaleev said.

"Come, come. Surely you don't you don't believe a dragon to be stupid, do you?"

"No, no. Of course not. A dragon is one of the smartest creatures ever created…" His voice trailed off for a moment. "And what do you mean noisey?" He said. Kaleev prided himself on being very quiet on his feet. There was a snort of to his right, behind a small rise. He heard Patearum's laugh in his head as he crept over the rise. "If you are the dragon, the vampire was riding, then show yourself so that we may get acquainted."

"To prove yourself worthy of the ride, you must find me."
The dragon said.

Kaleev jumped over the rise, expecting to be face to face
with the dragon. He was startled to be just a few feet from a
thousand-pound boar, who was rooting around the bottom of
the gully, searching for grub worms. Startled, the boar, with his
head already low and foot long tusks angled in Kaleev's
direction, charged at full speed. Still in shock that he hadn't
found the dragon, Kaleev stumbled over a log while trying to
back pedal out of the boar's way. The angry animal was almost
on top of him already.

The roar made the hair across all of Kaleev's body stand
on end. Where the boar had just been was now a flurry of mud,
leaves and moss. There was a sharp squeal near the opening to
the gully.

Kaleev got back to his feet and eased back into the
clearing just as Patearum was chewing up and swallowing the
last of the boar.

"You used ME?!" Kaleev practically screamed. Patearum,
unfazed by his outburst, glanced over in his direction.

"I didn't use you… Directly. I just needed a distraction
and I must say, you did an excellent job. Thank you."

"You used me as bait!" He retorted.

"Well, you see it your way, I'll see it mine." She said.

That boar was BIG. He thought.

"And I was hungry." She said in his head.

"Would you please stop doing that?" he said out loud.
"It's kind of strange having your voice in my head."

"Fine." She spoke out loud again.

When she stood to her full height in front of him, he
could see that from the ground to the top of her horns, was
about thirty feet. The tip of her snout to the end of her tail was
probably forty feet and her wing span was at least fifty feet. The

razor-sharp talons on her feet were impressive, to say the least. She had layers of blue-green scales that covered her from head to tail and even around the edges of her wings.

"Well, I found you! So, how about that ride?" He was slowly walking toward her. Unsure of how she'd react.

She had seen elves before. But something about this one felt different to her. Other than his white hair, when all others were black. He had a certain kind of confidence about him. She could tell it wasn't the kind rooted in arrogance or ignorance. Especially for an elf of five and a half feet in height.

She lowered her head to him, when he approached, as he lifted his hand to her. He placed his hand on her head just behind her ear. Instantly his thoughts were hers and hers became his. Then everything went black for Kaleev.

When he came to, he was looking up through the trees. He sat up slowly holding his head. "What the heck was that?" He said.

"It is what my race calls The Zampuant. It is mind sharing. You now have all of my wisdom and I have all of yours. Strange though… as that was the first time it's ever happened to me."

"What do you mean the first time for you? You had a rider before."

"Yes, but I've never had that happen before… Until now." She looked up and noticed the sun was rising. It was already morning. "Do you smell that?"

"Smell what?" He said. Just as he caught the scent of smoke. "That is not a camp fire."

"Come on." She said lowering her head to him so he could climb onto the saddle on her back.

"what are these long leather ropes on the back of your saddle for?"

"Oh… Those are for tying yourself into the saddle."

"Why would you tie yourself into the saddle?" he said.

Just then she leapt high into the air, spread her wings and with one powerful flap, they were above the trees. Already soaring high.

Collecting himself and the reins, he said. "Now I know what the ropes are for." With a laugh from the dragon, they were off towards the smoke.

Chapter 6

Patearum saw the plume of smoke just before Kaleev. "Over there." She said.

"I see it." he answered her.

As Patearum angled herself toward the smoke, and arrow streaked past her head. Kaleev leapt high into the air off of her back in an attempt to grab the arrow. Patreaum circled back, just as he was starting his freefall toward the ground and landed back in the saddle.

"Who the heck would be shooting arrows at us?" She asked.

"That would be my sister."

"Well, tell her to stop!"

"I will." He said. "Let's just land in that small clearing over there."

"Okay." She said. Folding her wings slightly, she glided in low and landed smoothly with all the precision and grace a creature like her should.

Kaleev jumped from her back and took of down a game trail toward the smoke. I hope everyone is alright he thought to himself as he rounded a large boulder. When he cleared the corner headed toward the stream, he stopped dead in his tracks.

"Good morning Kaleev. I see you have arrived safely." Said Myrith, the warlock. He was just standing there looking at Kaleev.

"Yes, thank you." He said, with a puzzled look on his face. "What are you doing here?"

"Your father summoned me." He replied.

"We better not keep him waiting."

"Are you bringing your dragon?" Myrith said angling his head to look over Kaleev's shoulder.

"How did you… Never mind. No, father doesn't know about her yet.

"Well, I advise you tell him as soon as possible." Myrith said. "And what do you mean her? Take me to her."

"What about my father?" Kaleev asked.

"He can wait a few more moments." The warlock said, walking past Kaleev down the trail he'd just arrived on.

When the pair entered the clearing with Kaleev in the lead, Patearum looked over his shoulder at the newcomer.

"Who do we have here?" She asked.

"This is Myrith, the warlock. He is a great friend of my family and of my kind." Kaleev replied.

"Well then, I am happy to meet you." Patearum said.

"And I, you." The warlock replied.He was staring at the dragon intently.

"Is there something wrong?" she asked Myrith.

“No, no. Nothing.” He said out loud. He thought to himself. There are no other dragons like this one. She has to be HER daughter. In all my years and the hundreds of dragons I’ve seen, none have been as beautiful as this one. All the others have been black, red or brown. “So how are you going to tell your father about her?” Myrith asked as her turned and headed back toward the smoke. Kaleev and Patearum followed along behind him. Myrith kept looking back to make sure she was still there. For a dragon, walking through the forest, I would’ve expected more noise.

“I’m sure he will see her coming.” Kaleev said. They walked about a half a mile along the edge of the stream. Rounding a moss-covered rock, they entered the clearing where Kaleev’s house had been. Myrith waved his hand and what fires were still burning, were extinguished in an instant. “What the…” Kaleev stopped mid thought as he took in the carnage in front of him.

The house was a smoldering pile of ash. The trees were singed or completely gone. There were some charred remains of what looked to be some kind of soldier, although he didn’t recognize any of the armor or weaponry that was still intact.

“Kaleev, Myrith! What is the meaning of this!?” Hugo shouted pointing his battle axe at the dragon with nothing but rage on his face.

“Father, let me explain.” Kaleev spoke to his father as he stepped in front of Patearum with his hands up, palms facing his father.

“Speak quickly boy!”

“She is mine.”

“YOURS?!” Hugo roared.

“Where are Merrita and Yanella?” Myrith asked trying to distance himself from confrontation boiling before him.

"Down by the stream. We need to go, now." Hugo said. "The Dragon stays here!" He shouted pointing a finger at Patearum.

"Fine!" said Kaleev. "She'll stay here." He turned to look at his dragon, giving her a reassuring smile.

I'll be fine. She said in his head.

The three of them headed down to the steam. Yanella was placing a damp cloth on Merrita's forehead when they arrived.

"Hey Kaleev, did you see that dragon I just took a shot at?" Yanella said.

Hugo, Myrith and Kallev had spoken about Merrita's wound on the way to the stream. Kaleev knelt down next to his mother and placed a hand on her forehead. "She' burning up." He said.

"Did you hear what I just said?" Yanella asked.

"Yes, Yan. I did." Kaleev had always called his sister by the pet name Yan. "We'll talk about that later."

Myrith and Hugo were speaking in whispsers when Kaleev returned to where they were standing. Myrith had been speaking "…he'll have to bring her over here."

"Bring who over here?" Kaleev asked

"Your dragon!" Hugo snapped sharply, still trying to whisper through his anger. "It seems we may have use for her."

"And what would that be?" Kaleev said shifting his gaze to the warlock.

The hint of a smile crept at the corner of Myrith's mouth. "Would you please go and get here? I will explain everything once she is here." Kaleev stared at the warlock another moment before he turned and started his jog back up the trail to where they had left his dragon.

"Yanella, Hugo. I will need certain roots and mosses." Looking at Hugo, he said. "You know the ones that I mean."

Hugo nodded and started off with Yanella toward the remains of what was their home.

Myrith knelt beside Merrita. Taking the cloth from her forehead and dipping in the stream to replace it back onto her head. Then he examined her wound. He thought to himself. If I'm right, then the dragon may be the key. He stood and waved his hand. A campfire, with a ring of small stones surrounding it, appeared out of nowhere and crackled to life.

Kaleev came walking into the clearing with Patearum a few steps behind him. Myrith left Merrita by the stream and walked over to the pair. He began explaining to them why, he believed, they needed the dragon there. That was when they heard Yanella's shout. "Step away from the dragon!"

When they all turned and looked her direction, they saw Yanella had her bow at full draw with an arrow already knocked. The tip of the arrow was trained on Patearum's head. Kaleev's sword was in his hand in an instant. "YAN! Put the bow down!"

"No! Kal, they rode in here on dragons! How do you think they were able to burn the house down and everything around it!? And they've almost KILLED mother with their poison!"

Myrith stepped in front of Kaleev and spoke in a calm voice, barely above a whisper, that resonated clearly through the clearing. "Yanella, please. Put down your bow. The dragon is here to help and only because I asked if she would help."

"Why?" Yanella said. "How can it help?"

"Lower your weapon and let me try to explain."

"Fine!" She said. Finally lowering here bow.

As she approached, Myrith put his arm around her shoulder and led her back toward the fire he'd created. Hugo walked into to camp carrying an arm full of moss, ginger and ginseng roots. Myrith reached into on of the invisible pockets inside his robes and produced and small pot. He placed the pot over the fire, where it floated all on its own.

Yanella filled the pot with water. Myrith said to put the roots in the pot and lay the moss next to Merrita. Hugo followed the instructions, placing the roots in the pot of boiling water. He returned to his wife and sat down with her, placing the moss next to her.

Patearum, who was clearly not surprised or scared of anything she'd seen so far, had curled up and lain down across from the fire where Myrith was. Kaleev was leaning back against her. Taking the moment to rest. Myrith poured some powder into to the water, which made it boil faster and turn bright blue. As the water boiled away it left a paste in the bottom of the pot. He took a wooden spoon made of oak and stirred what was left in the pot. He removed the pot from the fire and approached Patearum. "Now my dear, for your contribution… A dragon's tear."

She lifted her head and he placed the pot underneath it. She tilted her head just as a large tear slid down her face dripping off her cheek. The tear dropped right into the center of the pot. Myrith picked the pot back up and began to stir as he walked back over to where Merrita was laying.

"What does the tear do?" Yanella asked.

"The dragon's tear has properties in it that I believe will draw out the poison." Myrith explained. He spread the mixture over Merrita's wound and placed the moss over the top to protect it. "Now, we wait."

Now that night was quickly approaching. Yanella went back to the remains of the house. When she returned, she had managed to find some deer jerky, ginseng tea and some bread that hadn't been charred. "Well," Myrith said "let's eat. Then get some rest and we'll see how Merrita is doing in the morning."

Chapter 7

Merrita woke to the sounds of conversation between Myrith and Kaleev.

"… You have to understand Kaleev." Myrith was saying. "Your father has good reason to be mad. He is… scared for you."

"Scared for me? My father is scared of nothing."

"I know it seems that way but, let me tell you a story." Said Myrith.

"Your father had an experience once. Like you did with Patearum. Only it was with Patearum's mother. You see, only female dragons can experience Zampuant. The males are unable to do so. That is why you must not go and tell everyone about your mind share with Patearum." Myrith said.

"Patearum's mother, Maleea, gave her life in defense of Hugo. After Withella lured them into a trap, meant to kill the both of them." Myrith continued.

"It's true…" Merrita said in almost a whisper. Kaleev spun to see his mother propping herself on her elbows.

"Mother! You're awake!" Kaleev exclaimed.

"Yes, yes Kaleev, but you must listen to Myrith." Merrita took a deep breath and sighed. "Myrith, please continue."

"Maleea and Hugo were flying to the King's aid. Or so they were led to believe. You see, the King had gone on a hunt with his personal guard. They weren't hunting for anything in particular. The King just loved to be outdoors." Said Myrith.

"They were headed north. Now, mind you Kaleev, the dragon king and the elven king were alies." Myrith said. "Yet, there was a group of dragons, lead by the current king of the dragons, Withella. They were trying to create a rift between the two kings."

"Withella had lead a small group of dragons to the south to set up an ambush. While Tiina, his mate, headed north to attack the elven king and his guards.Tiina was killed in the confrontation. This sent Withella into a rage. The elven king sent one of his men to retrieve reinforcements.

"That man was intercepted and killed by the dragons. A dragon was sent in place of the guard. The Dragon delivered the message that the king had been attacked. But, the dragon told them the attacked had happened to the south.

"It was at this time that Hugo, on the back of Maleea, raced south, to aid the elven king. When they had arrived at the location, the dragon had indicated, they were immediately attacked.

"They were still 30 feet off the ground when they were slammed into by two of Withella's followers. Hugo was thrown from the saddle and into a grove of trees. At that time Hugo favored a Mezzita wood shield that he used to help break his fall. Breaking off many branches on his way down. Hugo still hit the ground hard, which put him in a daze.

"Maleea grabbed one of the dragons by the neck and whipped her head sharply to the right. Tearing the other dragons head completely off. She immediately searched for Hugo. Quickly finding the spot where he had landed. Just as she turned to fly down to him, she was hit with a fiery blast from behind.

"Spinning in midair, she slashed at the red dragon, catching him in the eyes, blinding him instantly. Looking over her shoulder she spotted Withella, closing in on Hugo. He had regained his footing and was wielding his shield and sword at the ready.

"Withella had realized that he had underestimated Hugo. Yet, it wasn't until after he had used his height over the elf to strike down at his head and take a bite. Only to return with a deep cut below one of his eyes.

"Maleea was roaring as she turned her whole body toward Hugo. Causing her not to see the four dragons creeping from the tree line she had just been facing. When the next blast of fire came, it hit her with its full force. Propelling her toward Withella and Hugo.

"Withella twisted out of her path as she smashed into the grove where Hugo had just been moments before. Hugo rushed to her side. 'MALEEA!' He yelled. 'Are you alright?'

'I'm not… doing so good… you?' She responded. She climbed back to her feet, staring into the faces of the five dragons who wanted nothing more than to kill them. Maleea spoke quietly, not breaking eye contact with the angry dragons.

'This was not the reception I had in mind. Hugo, you must run. Get out of here! The fire they are breathing is laced with sulfer, making it five times hotter than normal. If they fire on us, that shield of yours will do nothing to protect you.

'I'm not going anywhere without you!' Hugo said. She could hear the red dragons drawing in their breath. So, she did the only thing she could think of. She used here huge claws to quickly dig a long hole in the ground. She grabbed Hugo and threw him into it, laying down on top of it to cover the hole.

"Hugo screamed at her. 'MALEEA! NOOOOOO!... No! Let me fight them with you!' Just then the space he occupied became very hot. He could see the flames lapping through the gaps between the dirt and Maleea's body. The heat was so strong that it became hard to breath and he blacked out."

"When I came to. I knew she was gone. Though I didn't want to believe it." Hugo said as he walked into the camp.

"Hugo," Said Myrith. "I'm sorry old friend."

"Don't apologize Myrith. It was past time that they knew." He paused for a moment. Seeming lost in the memory. "I felt as though someone had ripped half of my mind out, half my soul even. I dug myself out from where she had covered me." A tear was rolling down his face. "They burned her alive… She never moved. Not even for a moment, not even to save her own life!"

He sat down next to Merrita, who gave him a reassuring look and placed her arm around him. Myrith looked pointedly at Kaleev.

"This is why you must keep quiet about her." He said nodding his head to indicate Patearum. Who appeared to be sound asleep.

"You could be very powerful with her at your side." Said Hugo. "But I don't know if you're ready for that kind of responsibility. Your mother was the only one, after that experience, who was able to pull me from the fog of confusion that had settled over me. She was who had helped me be able to cope with the loss."

Patearum looked up from where she layed and said. "So, my mother, who was killed by Withella, was your protector?"

Hugo got to his feet and walked over to her. Passing by Yanella and Myrith without even a glance. He said. "Your mother was my great friend and companion. She had some of the greatest fighting instincts of any dragon I have ever known! And yes, I guess you could say, I loved her for that."

No one spoke for a time. "Well," Myrith said. "I have looked at Merrita's wound. The tear I received from Patearum has surrounded the poison and will keep it from spreading. But we will need to return her to Gavalonia as soon as possible."

"The Blooms?" Hugo asked.

"Yes." Myrith replied. "The Mezzita Blooms will be able to draw the poison out of the wound, curing her and healing the wound."

"What are we waiting for then?" Yanella said. "Gather your supplies. Let's go"

"Not so fast Yanella." Myrith said. "In order to get there, we have to get to the Space Tear. That is not easy to do. And it appears we are walking."

"You know," Hugo started. "We could go to the village and buy some horses for the trip."

"That's a good idea but, Patearum won't be able to come. The villagers wouldn't be able to understand that she's not a threat." Said Myrith.

"That's okay," Said Kaleev. "Patearum and I can fly to the small lake on the other side of the village and wait for you."

"I think that will work." Said Hugo. "Just make sure you're not seen."

"Okay dad, okay."

“I will make sure we do not get into any trouble.” Patearum said looking crossways at Kaleev.

“Kal?” Yaneela said.

“Yes Yan, what is it?” Kaleev turned to see Yanella had already covered the distance between them and was standing next to him and the dragon.

“Can I… umm… Can I go with you and Patearum?” She said looking up at the dragon with a sympathetic look on her face. Patearum lowered her head to look Yanella is the face, eye to eye and softly said.

“As long as you promise to stop shooting arrows at us.”

“I do promise.” Yanella replied immediately.

“Good.” Said Patearum. “Then let’s go.”

Yanella didn’t think dragons were able to smile. But the look on Patearums face said something completely different.

Chapter 8

The dark leader of the vampires, Lord Loceirn, sat on his throne. Pondering his next move. They had found the crystals deep within the planet and had, accidently, awoken Withella in the process. What a stroke of luck, he thought to himself. I have the crystals being fashioned into amulets to allow my army to travel in the sunlight. Which would have killed them all, had it been attempted before. And, I've managed to strike a deal with the dragon king, that black hearted devil. He wanted to kill Ingio Hugonovs so badly… A three-foot-long white scar on the pitch-black face of a dragon does tend to stand out.

"I sent two armed parties through the ancient Space Tear. One, to bring back more humans for us to feed on. And two, to retrieve the Elf Kings daughter, Yanella and kill The Protector and his family!" He was shouting. "Well, it looks like both endeavors failed. The Kingdom of light could have been mine so easily!" Slamming his fist on the arm of the throne, showing his full frustration.

The grip of his other hand was on the top of the traitor's head, causing a great deal of pain. You could tell by the look on the man's face. The guards on either side of Loceirn's throne glanced at each other, knowing what was coming.

Loceirn's grip tightened slightly and with a violent twist of his hand, he broke the traitor's neck. He kept twisting until the head came completely off.

"Drain his body of the human blood." He barked. "no sense in letting it go to waste." As his smirk changed into a full smile. "See, my children!" He shouted. "That is what happens when you betray this clan!" He tossed the head deep into the crowded gathering hall to the roars of delight at the spectacle. He continued to the crowd.

"I had doubts that this clan would survive… But with this new food supply," he indicated with a wave of his hand. A couple of the guards to his right removed the fabric draping over the cage. Inside were eight humans from the village that Kaleev had visited earlier. There was a swell in the noise as the cheer rose throughout the chamber. The cage was small enough that all the humans could do was squirm around in terror.

"These creatures are called 'Humans.' They are from a planet called 'Earth.' And might I add that their blood is intoxicatingly superb. It is unlike anything I have ever tasted." Loceirn boasted. A voice from the crowed carried over the noise.

"What about their sun? Doesn't the like from it kill us?"

"This is true… But I have a plan. We will be able to harvest these creatures and bring them here for you. My CLAN!" Loceirn said as another roar of approval erupted from the crowd. "Their planet has what they call 'Night' and 'Day.' The Night time is when their sun doesn't shine. THAT is when we will hunt them. They are slow and clumsy. They cannot see in the dark, which will cause them to be scared of us.

"During the day is when we will rest. While their sun is high in the sky, we will be deep underground and safe from the light." Another voice called out.

"What about the Elves?"

"Yes… The Elves… I have a plan for them as well. They will not be able to interfere once my plan is complete. They will have no choice but to allow us our plunder!" As he finished speaking he waved his hand again. But this time it was toward the throne. Behind the throne were two huge doors that ran the full fifty feet from the floor to the ceiling. As they were being pulled open a hush fell over the crowd. They all stared into the darkness and the silence was replaced by a deep, heavy breath being drawn in and let out.

Some of the vampires noticed the large red glowing orbs near the ceiling. Pretty soon all the eyes in the chamber were fixed to those orbs. The silence was deafening. With an evil grin on his face Loceirn spoke quietly.

"The key to any confrontation is to have the upper hand. With that being said," his words now increasing in volume and pitch. "May I introduce… OUR KEY!"

The two red orbs slowly began to descend from the ceiling and move forward. Some of the vampires were beginning to understand that they were looking at eyes of an obviously huge creature. But his size truly didn't begin to sink in until they heard the single step, the dragging of the tail, and the roar.

The roar shook the pillars of the hall. Dust began falling from the joints and cracks in the ceiling. The sound vibrated through every vampire to their very core. Most took a step back in shock while others stood still in terror. Almost petrified into place by the sound.

"Do not be alarmed!" Loceirn Shouted. "Withella is a friend and ally. He will remove the Elves from our lives FOREVER!"

The vampires who had been screaming in terror began to scream with joy. Once the announcement had settled through the ones frozen in place, they found their voices again and joined in the cheering.

Chapter 9

"The air is a lot colder up here." Yanella said. Staring over Kaleev's shoulder at the ground far, far below.

"We have to remain this high, so as not to be noticed by the villagers." Kaleev said. "Patearum, let's land behind that rock formation to the right of the lake. The rocks will hide or presence."

"Okay, hang on." Patearum replied. She dropped out of the scattered clouds. Swooping in low over the lake she dipped one of her legs into the water. When she pulled her leg back out there was a nice sized trout trapped in her claw. She came around for the landing and touched down lightly as to create as little noise as possible. Yanella and Kaleev went t o work setting up their camp. Kaleev collected firewood while Yanella refilled their water skins from the lake.

When Kaleev returned with the wood he'd collected, he looked over at Patearum. Who was munching happily on the 50 pound trout she'd snatched out of the water.

"I don't understand how you can eat that raw." He said with a shiver. She looked over at him. Then she tossed the rest of the fish in the air, puffed out a small flame, which seared the fish, and caught it back in her mouth. She finished the fish with a loud gulp.

"There, how's that?" She said.

"Well… You didn't save any for Yan and me."

"But I was hungry…" She said with a little sheepish look on her face. "You know, a large boar only lasts so long." With a wink she curled up like a dog again. Intent on taking a nap.

"Hey! How about a little help with the fire?"

She opened one eye and blew out a puff of fire at the ring of stones, where he'd stacked the wood.

"There… Happy now?" She said.

"Overjoyed…" He muttered sarcastically. He went down towards to lake hoping he'd be able to catch some dinner.

Yanella was just finishing up with the water skins when she heard the snap of a twig. She whirled into a crouch, sword already in hand.

"A bit jumpy there, girly." Said an older woman who was standing in place. She was dressed in a grey cloak with a dingy white dress underneath. She had an eye patch with a very strange symbol on it that Yanella didn't recognize. But, the most frightening thing was that she was standing right next to Yanella. The woman's gaze followed Yan's down to the creature, know as a Fennarious, standing next to the woman.

"Gorgeous, isn't he?" Said the woman.

"Who… Who are you?" Yan asked. Letting a little of the panic seep through her words.

"Oh yes! I almost forgot. My name is Alexandria. Sorceress of the vampire clan." As she spoke, her hand was stroking the fennarious behind the ears.

The tall tales, or so she'd thought, told by Hugo didn't even come close to describing the animal. If that's what you could call it. His head was the shape of a puma only about three times larger. His body was black as night. When he opened his maw. She saw the double row of teeth dripping with saliva. Yan took an involuntary step back at the sight. According to the stories a Fennarious' favorite meal was Elf meat.

Alexandria whispered something that Yanella couldn't make out. The animal crouched down on it's eight legs. Having four in the front and four in the back, this animal was considered the fastest creature to have existed, when on open ground. They were hunted to extinction by Yanella's elven ancestors, or so she thought.

"What do you want?" Asked Yan.

"Just for you to come with me, my dear." Alexandria replied.

"She is not going anywhere with you!"

Alexandria knew that voice. But it couldn't be. She saw him perish in the duel with the Wizard of Lockmoore. When she turned to her right, she saw him. Standing in the shadows of the trees. Myrith... she thought. There was a split second of shock on her face, then it was replaced with utter calm and indifference, then disgust.

"I saw you die!" She said.

"No... I let you think I was dead. But I can assure you that I am very much alive. I see you've sold out the human race to those monsters." He said.

"They pay very well and provide me with whatever I need." Placing her hand on the back of the fennarious.

"That foul creature needs to be destroyed!" Myrith said pointing at the fennarious.

"Oh, come now. He's Beautiful." She said.

"More like pure evil." He spat back in reply.

Her look of disgust turned to rage and her arm came up in an instant. A bolt of lightning shot from her hand striking Myrith squarely in the chest. The Fennarious launched himself towards Yanella. The creature was instantly blindsided by a diving Hugo. The Fennarious and Hugo were rolling and churning up dust near the waters edge. Hugo broke free, rolling to one knee behind his dragon shield. His back to Yanella. The beast rolled to his feet, shook his head and dropped into a crouch with the cold look of death on his face. With a blood curdling roar the creature launched himself again. Striking Hugo's shield with such force, it knocked Hugo down underneath his shield. Which was a good thing since the beast couldn't get to Hugo through the shield.

"Lightning bolts? That's the best you could come up with?" Myrith said as he got back to his feet, still smoldering. He readjusted his robe with a shake, all of the ash falling away, to reveal a cloak of midnight blue with shimmering stars. All the while walking into the clearing.

"That robe… THAT ROBE! There is no way you beat him!" Alexandria exclaimed.

"Oh, but on the contrary, Alexandria. I did beat him and he is… No more."

The roar had awoken Patearum. "Kaleev?" She said. Then the panic set in. Kaleev?! She thought. In her mind she heard his voice say.

Patearum, I'm fine. But we need to help the others.

Okay, what do you want me to do? She asked.

I need you to roar. Kaleev said. As soon as he thought the words, he launched himself from his hiding spot behind Alexandria, in a cluster of boulders.

Alexandria heard the roar and felt the hair on the back of her neck stand on end. She'd heard a dragon's roar before. But they didn't sound anything like this.

Myrith, seeing the look on her face, said. "You might meet her. If you survive this duel."

"Survive?!" She screamed. "You must have forgotten Myrith. I was the one who trained the Wizadr of Lockmoore. But I didn't teach him every spell or incantation I know!"

Kaleev reached the fennarious a second before Yanella. The beast dropped to its belly just as the two elves with glowing swords got to him. Kaleev saw the animal drop down and tried to slow his momentum, but it carried him right past his target. Yanella, too, was carried past her target due to her momentum. All the while Hugo was struggling to his feet. The weight of the animal had taken a lot of energy to resist. The creature lunged at

Hugo again. Only to be hit by a solid beam of bright cobalt blue light.

The beam of light, which came from Myrith, carried the animal right to the waters edge. Where it landed in a heap. Alexandria, infuriated, shot a bolt of lightning at the nearest elf, Kaleev. Kaleev saw the bolt coming but couldn't get his feet to move fast enough. At the last second, he brought his sword up as his only line of defense. He held the sword squarely in front of him, glowing green as ever. He squeezed his eyes shut, bracing himself for the impact.

In the same moment he was expecting to feel the blast, he felt a sudden rush of air instead. Patearum landed in front of him, deflecting the lightning with her heavily scaled body. She swung her head around and roared at the fennarious who was scrambling to his feet.

"Oh… My God… It… Can't be… Can't be her. I saw that egg destroyed…" Alexandria said. More to herself than anyone else. She called the fennarious, which was by her side in a flash. "This is not over Myrith!" In a flash of light, Alexandria and the creature were gone.

Myrith walked over to Hugo. "Are you alright, old friend?"

"Yes, yes. I'm fine. That was most interesting, don't you think?" Hugo looked at Myrith who was watching Yanella sheathing her sword.

"And that is why we must return. Along with finding the cure for Merrita." Myrith said to Hugo. "You and I will go down to the village." Myrith look over at Kaleev. "keep a close eye on your sister."

"Wait, wait. Please Myrith." Kaleev replied. "You and father can head down to the village in the morning."

"Alright… Alright. We will rest tonight and travel to the village in the morning."

Kaleev knew the lightning from Alexandria had to have taken a toll on Myrith. He felt better now that Myrith had agreed to rest for the evening.

"Patearum?" Kaleev asked.

"Yes, Kaleev?" She replied.

"Do you think you think you could catch another trout for the rest of us to eat?"

"If you ask nicely." She said with a sly grin.

"What if I asked nicely, Patearum?" Myrith interjected.

"Well then." She answered. "I shall return with two trouts."

Then she looked at Myrith. If a dragon could look surprised, Myrith would've seen it on her face in that moment.

"How long have you been able to understand me or my kind?" She asked.

Chapter 10

"From the first time we met." Myrith said with his own sly grin.

"So, you could've told Kaleev and I?" She said.

"No, no, no. That would've ruined the surprise. And for a wizard surprise is everything."

"You are definitely full of surprises." With a push from her powerful legs, she shot into the air and was gone with a woosh. The others made their way back to camp and checked on Merrita, who was sleeping Peacefully.

"Well," Hugo said. "At least she is getting some rest."

"As should the rest of us." Myrith said.

"What about a look out?" Kaleev wondered out loud.

"There's no need when you have a dragon." Hugo replied.